Step-by-Step Author Website Guide

Workbook Edition

Tyora Moody

Tymm Publishing LLC
Columbia, SC

Published by Tymm Publishing LLC
701 Gervais Street, Suite 150-185
Columbia, SC 29201
TymmPublishing.com

ISBN-13: 978-0998456935
ISBN-10: 0998456934

Cover Design: TywebbinCreations.com
Editing: Flora Brown

The Literary Entrepreneur

Ebooks & Workbooks

The Literary Entrepreneur's Toolkit

The Literary Entrepreneur's Toolkit- Workbook Edition

Step-by-Step Author Website Guide

Step-by-Step Author Website Guide – Workbook Edition

Freebies & Email Courses
www.theliteraryentrepreneur.com

Instagram Marketing for Authors: Free 5-Day Email Course

Twitter Marketing for Authors: Free 5-Day Email Course

Table of Contents

Introduction

While working on *The Literary Entrepreneur's Toolkit — Second Edition*, I realized there was a lot more I could add about author websites. After much consideration, I decided it was best to fully expand on this topic in a separate book, the *Step-by-Step Author Website Guide*.

You see I believe an author's website is the **center of their book marketing**, especially when you want to establish authority in your field, build a robust mailing list or provide unique experiences for your readers. If you're wondering where my expertise on author websites comes from, let me introduce my background to you.

In 1999, an author approached me back during my web design hobby days. She just released a new book and needed a website. That was the beginning of my web design business. I've been working with authors for over fifteen years - both traditional and self-published. In 2010, I personally crossed over to being an author. So, I've seen two sides to designing a website, for clients and myself.

I love working with authors in the beginning stages, so I'm especially delighted to help new authors who chose to purchase this book. If you're published and already have a website, but you know that your website needs help, then this book is for you as well.

I also have seen how website platforms have evolved over the years and the choices can be mind-boggling. Creating a DIY website even with drag n' drop is not ideal for everyone. It helps to have an eye for design.

I plan to assist you through the process, so you will have a professional website that works well for you and your readers.

Do I Really Need a Website?

I always tell authors, when it comes to branding, the brand starts with YOU. Your name is on the book cover. When readers see your name, what do you hope they will be saying? Even more importantly, where do you think they may go to find out more about you.

We hope they go to Amazon first and search our name, right? That's what we all want... book sales. *Cha-ching!*

Amazon does a great job giving space to authors via an Amazon Central page, but a true fan may want more. Amazon is not the only store of choice. They dominate, but don't forget Barnes & Nobles, iBook, Kobo, etc., all still exist. There are multiple channels.

The same way you leave work each day to head home, you need a solid home on the internet. The number one search engine remains Google. When a reader is searching for more information about you, it's ideal that your home (your website) tops the search results.

I often study author's social media profiles and notice they depend too much on sending readers to their Facebook or Twitter page. That's not cool to me, mainly because a professional website should be the center of your online presence. It's the one central location that you own. Notice that word OWN. No matter how great the features are on a Facebook page, there are limits to that page. Each of these social media networks has their own terms of usage and rules, which can and will change often.

How many times have you gone to your Facebook page and noticed it looked slightly different? Did that frustrate you? I always laugh when I see people complaining about interface changes. It's a free website and the Facebook CEO, Mark Zuckerberg, can dictate what he wants or at least what his FB Shareholders want (Google: NASDAQ:FB).

There is nothing more beautiful, in my opinion, than a clean, well-organized professional website. First impressions are important and even more so in this fast-paced world.

It's important to not simply throw a website together. Just as fast as a visitor enters your website, they can exit. What you don't want is a "hot mess" as Niecey Nash, host of *Clean House* (2003–2010) on the Style Network, would say to the owner of a cluttered home.

How To Use This Workbook

Since the release of *The Literary Entrepreneur's Toolkit,* many people have told me how much they like to highlight and make notes in that book. The *Step-by-Step Author Website Guide – Workbook Edition* provides an organized way to keep your notes together.

There are worksheets that walk you through how to:

- Select the best hosting options

- Prepare your website budget

- Define your author brand

- Create the essentials pages you need to build your website

- Consider the benefits of blogging

- Attract readers to your website

Step 1: Domain Name

The same way you have a mailing address, you need an easy to remember web address. This starts with investing in a domain name. It's heartbreaking to me to see business owners who use a free web host, but don't even take the time to invest in a domain name. If you are on a budget, it's not hard to forward a domain name to your free web hosting. The fees are usually small. Having a domain name on your business cards and social media profiles speak volumes to your credibility.

How to Select A Domain Name

If you are an author, the domain name is usually yourname.com. For branding purposes, it's always best to use your name or your pen name.

When you do a domain name search, sometimes the name you want may be taken so it's good to have a list of alternatives. For example, one of my author clients Monique Miller wanted moniquemiller.com for her domain name, but it was already taken at the time. She opted for authormoniquemiller.com. A few years later, she was able to obtain the domain name of her choice.

As you explore domain names think about whether people will have a hard time spelling your name or if someone shares your name. Author Tia McCollors ran into this issue and uses not only TiaMcCollors.com, but also TiaWrites.com. Both domain names are directed to her author website.

Author Stacy Hawkins Adams was smart enough to realize that her first name, "Stacy" could also be spelled "Stacey." She purchased her main domain name, stacyhawkinsadams.com AND staceyhawkinsadams.com for those just in case moments.

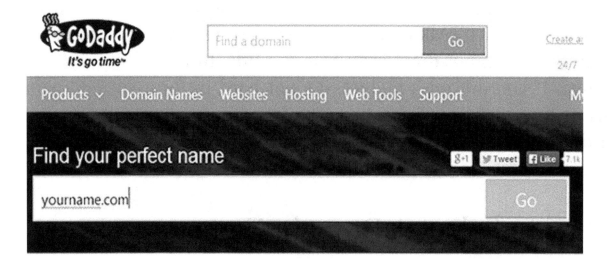

Now that you have your list of possible domain names, here are a few of the most popular registrars:

- Domain – http://www.domain.com
- Godaddy – http://www.godaddy.com
- Register – http://www.register.com

After you choose a registrar, type in your domain name to check for the name's availability. There are other extensions like ".net," ".tv," ".us," etc, but ".com" is preferred.

I have had many non-techie clients successfully do this process on their own, but I do want to take a moment to let you know that there are web design and web hosting companies that will take care of all of this for you. I think it's always a good idea to understand what you are purchasing and why. I've always told clients to purchase these items on their own so that they can be sure they are the "owner" of the domain name, which is very important.

Now if the domain name of your choice is available, I recommend (1) purchasing for more than a year and (2) setting the payment renewal on automatic. Many people have lost ownership of domain names by missing the renewal window. When you see an email from your domain registrar, pay attention. I had an experience where my credit card expired, so the renewal didn't go through. Yikes! I'm so glad I stay on top of my email.

One other piece of advice, if you have multiple domain names, keep all of them at the same registrar. It's just easier to manage them in one location.

Selecting a Domain Name

1a. List a few domain choices below with the first one being your preferred domain name.

Option 1 _____

Option 2 _____

Option 3 _____

Option 4 _____

Option 5 _____

1b. Record and compare pricing from domain companies.

Name of Company	Cost per year
	$
	$
	$
	$
	$

1c. Is it cost-savings for you to purchase more than one year at a time?

❏ Yes

❏ No

1d. Did you select auto-renewal?

❏ Yes

❏ No

Domain Name Final Cost: $_____

Step 2: Web Hosting

Web hosting or hosting is just as important as the domain name. When you pay for hosting you're basically renting space online for your website files to sit for the whole world to see.

Free Hosting

Now if you have some HTML and/or graphic skills, you can probably create or find a template for your website. I'm a WordPress gal, so I highly recommend trying out the self-hosted WordPress.org.

If you think you don't have time to build a website and you don't have the budget for a web designer, any of these free hosting sites will work initially.

- **Blogger** – http://www.blogger.com
- **Weebly** – http://www.weebly.com

- **Wix** – http://www.wix.com
- **WordPress** – http://www.wordpress.com

Please do consider purchasing the domain name and pay the extra fee to connect the domain to the free hosting. This is worth the investment.

Paid Hosting Plans

As a literary entrepreneur, I'm always going to highlight from a business aspect the importance of ownership. While free hosting involves the least amount of investment, a paid hosting plan allows a business owner more freedom to customize and have control over their own website.

With this type of hosting, you will (1) need to hire a web designer to build your website or (2) build the website yourself using a platform like self-hosted wordpress.org or another option (I will discuss in Step 3).

Since WordPress is so popular, most hosting companies offer "WordPress Hosting." This means that WordPress is installed for you and you just need to customize the installation for your needs.

Here are some recommended hosting companies (these are NOT affiliate links) that offer WordPress hosting as well as other paid hosting plans.

- **Dreamhost** – http://www.dreamhost.com

- **Godaddy** – http://www.godaddy.com
- **Hostgator** – http://www.hostgator.com

Most companies like godaddy.com allow you to purchase both the domain name and hosting. If you are a person who likes to keep their billing in one place, this may work for you.

If you decide to register your domain name at one company and purchase hosting at the other (this is what I have done), there is another step that involves changing the DNS Servers or Domain Nameservers. The DNS Server is what connects your domain name to your webhosting.

Examples of DNS Nameservers (there will usually be two):

Godaddy.com
ns01.domaincontrol.com, ns02.domaincontrol.com

Hostgator.com
ns3599.hostgator.com, ns3600.hostgator.com

For more information about how DNS Servers work visit, How Stuff Works at http://computer.howstuffworks.com/dns.htm

If this is making your head spin, purchase both the domain name and webhosting at the same company. It's the easiest route.

Premium or Subscription Hosting

When I wrote The *Literary Entrepreneur's Toolkit* back in 2013, I was vaguely aware of what I'm calling Premium or Subscription Hosting. This is the one-stop shop where you receive:

- Domain registration
- Hosting
- Templates for building your website
- Extra storage space
- No ads, if you upgrade from free service

Some platforms that include Premium or Subscription hosting include a few already mentioned.

Weebly.com users can upgrade starting at $8 per month. Users have access to unlimited storage, no ads, and advanced statistics.

Wix.com offers free hosting, but you can upgrade to remove ads, obtain more storage, unlimited pages, and more templates. Pricing begins at $10 per month.

WordPress.com offers premium hosting as well. If you really don't want to go the route of working with a self-hosted installation, which does have a learning curve, for an investment of $8.25 per month, you can have access to much more than the free version of WordPress.

Squarespace.com offers very sophisticated templates as well as the ability to create beautiful online e-commerce stores. The e-commerce is really what sets this platform apart from the others. They start at $12 per month if paid annually for a personal website. If you prefer not to pay annually, pricing starts at $16 per month.

If you do want the ability to have your own online store, Squarespace websites use SSL security which is highly recommended by Google. This simple means that your URL would be **https://** – which is considered secure for passing sensitive information like credit card information.

There are other options for adding an online store, and SSL certificates can be purchased separately if you plan to go that route. We will take a look at this a bit further when we discuss how you want to sell books from your author website.

WordPress.com vs. WordPress.org

Since I'm a Wordpress geek, a common question I receive is what's the difference between WordPress.com and WordPress.org? I wanted to address this before you make a decision on the type of hosting.

WordPress.com probably provides the best selection of themes and features for those who sign-up as members. With the ability to create pages, it's not hard to create a simple website alongside a blog using free hosting. Domain name forwarding and very simple customization are offered for an annual fee. The platform is really excellent, but like any free service, there are limitations. As stated above, you can also upgrade to the premium hosting.

WordPress.org is for self-hosted websites or blogs. To download and install WordPress is free. The software is open-source, meaning that tons of developers around the world have the opportunity to create products like themes and plugins. This is the beauty of using the self-hosted version of WordPress. Your world is open to thousands and thousands of features that you can use to create your very own customized version. You will need to invest in paid hosting or WordPress hosting (if you want the install done for you.)

Select a Web Hosting Solution

2a. List a few Web hosting solution below with the first one being your preferred choice.

Option 1 _____

Option 2 _____

Option 3 _____

Option 4 _____

Option 5 _____

2b. Record and compare pricing from Web hosting.

On the next page, make note if its easier for you to make payments per month or annually. Which is more cost-effective for you?

Name of Company	Cost per mth	Cost per yr
	$	$
	$	$
	$	$
	$	$
	$	$
	$	$
	$	$
	$	$
	$	$
	$	$

2c. Did you select auto-renewal?

❏ Yes

❏ No

Hosting Final Cost: $_____

I know many authors who have lost their domain names and websites because they let these expenses slip off their radar.

An author website is considered apart of your marketing so many of your recurring expenses can be tax-deductions later. *Please check with your accountant or tax preparer for confirmation.*

Use the *Website Recurring Expenses Worksheet* on the next page to record your expenses.

Website Recurring Expenses Worksheet

Total Website Costs

NOTE: Other rows have been added for other expenses that may come later like web design, mailing list provider, etc.

Expense	Cost per year
Domain Name	$
Hosting	$
Web Design	$
Mailing List Provider	$
Social Media Management	$
	$
	$
	$
	$
TOTAL:	$

Step 3: Your Website Design

You know the saying, "Don't judge a book by its cover" is cliché, but let's be honest, how often have you refused to pick up a book because something about the cover didn't suit your tastes. The same reaction happens with a website. You may have written an outstanding book, but if your website doesn't look the part, you could LOSE potential readers.

Before building your author website, it helps to define who is the target reader most likely to be interested in your book. I also wanted to take the time in this section to assist you with ideas you should consider before approaching a designer or before tackling the website DIY.

Define Your Author Brand Worksheet

It's important before sitting down with a designer or attempting to select a template that you understand your author brand.

3a. Do you write fiction or nonfiction?

_____

_____

_____

_____

3b. If you write fiction, which genre– romance, suspense, or fantasy?

_____

_____

_____

_____

3c. If you write nonfiction, is your book a memoir or self-help?

_____

_____

_____

_____

3d. Do you write in multiple genres? Both fiction and nonfiction? Do you have a major theme in your books (tagline).

_____

_____

_____

_____

_____

_____

_____

3e. What other authors share the readership that you're looking for to purchase your books?

_____

_____

_____

_____

_____

_____

_____

_____

_____

_____

Think Mobile

Did you know you could potentially lose a valuable visitor because they couldn't view your website on their mobile device? That's right, smartphones, tablets, and e-readers have grown in popularity. People like the convenience of pulling up websites on their mobile devices.

How often do you login to Facebook, Twitter or your email on a mobile device? If there is a link, you naturally want to click it to view more. This is where it's a bit more critical to pay attention to who you chose as a web designer or the theme you chose for your website.

Most websites using responsive web design (RWD) are built to adapt to being viewed on a desktop computer, a tablet or smartphone.

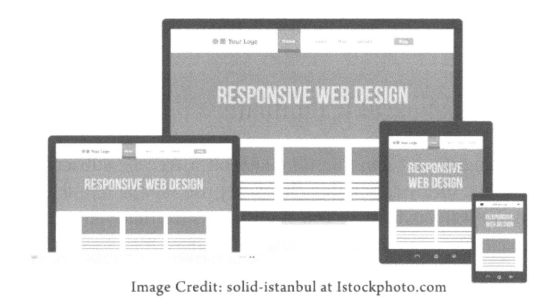

Image Credit: solid-istanbul at Istockphoto.com

I cover some elements to avoid on your website in the next section, but if you are one of those folks who like movement and a bit of flashiness to your website, iPhones and iPads have never supported Flash. Now Android is jumping on the bandwagon too. If you do want a bit of movement, an experienced web designer/developer can build some nifty effects with HTML5, CSS3, and JavaScript.

Bottom line, have the conversation with your web designer or check your chosen theme on a mobile device to see how it appears before you commit to using it for your website.

DIY Web Design

Many people choose the DIY method because it's cost effective. But is the decision time effective? It's important to think through your website's interface to avoid hours of frustration. There are two choices.

1. Select a manageable template.

While looking for a theme or template on a free or subscription hosting, make sure you not only choose a professional template but one that you can customize. You want to ensure that your website doesn't look like a hundred other sites that share the

same template too. I'm always disappointed to see the exact same theme I've seen elsewhere with no attention to branding.

Check to be sure you can at least change the banner and/or background image. A really good theme or template will allow you to customize most of these areas.

- banner or graphical top header
- sidebar(s)
- footer
- background image
- CSS (fonts, colors, etc.)

I see a lot of authors select templates based on the demos. Pay attention to the demo. Do you have enough content to build the website and keep a similar look? **Always start simple.** Websites should grow and you can always change to a more complex template later as your skills and content increase.

2. Learn web design.

If you really want to jump into designing a website yourself, but don't want to learn responsive web design from scratch, here are a couple of web design platforms to consider. If you have skills with Photoshop, the interfaces are very similar.

Webflow.com - You can build a really small website (2 pages) for free or invest $12 per month for more pages and storage

Adobe Dreamweaver or **Muse:** Either one of these programs can be purchased via the Creative Cloud individually at $14.99 per month or both (along with all apps) at $49.99 per month. This is going to be the highest end of DIY web design. Visit **Adobe.com**.

I worked with Dreamweaver for over a decade, but I started with learning the basics of HTML back in the late 1990's. It's a language that is relatively easy to learn, but these days you also need to learn CSS3 and sometimes javascript to build a website from scratch. I have not worked with Muse that much, but it has a very similar interface to Webflow if you prefer a more drag and drop environment.

Keep it Professional

If you saw something on someone else's website and you thought it was cute, try going back to the website a few times. Did you find yourself skipping over it or becoming annoyed? Keep those little annoyances in mind as I break down what you should not add to your website.

DO NOT add the following irritating things to your website unless you want to drive visitors away.

Flash intros, especially with no skip, should be avoided. Not just Flash intros, but websites that are entirely built in Flash are a big NO-NO! As I mentioned above, Flash does not work on most mobile devices.

Music that loads as soon as the visitor enters the page. Do you really want to scare an unsuspecting person with their speakers or headphones on away from your website?

Huge graphics with large file sizes. Okay, so there are not a lot of people using dial-up, but you still want to avoid affecting your website loading time or taking up too much real estate on a person's monitor.

Please limit the movement. No blinking animations. No scrolling text. People want information, don't make it difficult.

Large and/or unreadable fonts. Most browsers allow users to adjust the font size by using the (+) and (-) sign. Remember, this is a computer screen; you don't want people to strain their eyes trying to read your text.

Clashing colors schemes. Color is pretty important. I spend a lot of time whether I'm working on a book cover, bookmark or a website to make sure that the colors work for the author. If you are not sure what colors you want to use on your website, try checking out these resources below:

❏ Color Meanings in Design [Infographic]
   http://designspiration.net/image/3651587849394/

❏ The Psychology of Colors [Infographic]
   http://careyjolliffe.files.wordpress.com/2013/02/cjga-color-theory-3.jpg

❏ Colour Lovers
   http://www.colourlovers.com/colors

Website I Like Worksheet

You will probably want to spend some time searching for websites that share your niche or genre. Google some of author websites.

List at least 3-5 websites you like. Note what elements appealed to you.

Website I Like	What Did I Like

Contractor's Planning Sheet

If you want to hire a web designer or virtual assistant, let them know you've purchase a domain and your branding needs.

In some cases, these contractors will need to be sent a 1099. *Please consult with your accountant or tax preparer about using contractors and the current tax laws.*

To get started:

- ❐ Ask for referrals
- ❐ Google designers
- ❐ Look for local designers

Designer/Assistant Info	Notes (experience, costs, time, etc)

Web Design Planning Sheet

Do you have time to design this or will you need a designer/virtual assistant? Remember your time will be based on the type of hosting package you selected in Step 2.

❑ Yes

❑ No

If you purchased paid hosting where you need to add your own files, will you want to design the interface (Using HMTL, etc). If so:

❑ I will purchase a subscription for an online app (Webflow, Adobe Dreamweaver, Adobe Muse, etc.)

❑ I will take a class online or offline

❑ I purchased WordPress hosting and find a template (move to the next section for template options)

❑ I will hire a designer to handle the web design for me

If you purchase a subscription based hosting where there are template selections, you will want to take your time choosing a template that you can work with easily.

- ❑ I want to find a free ready-made template (WordPress, Wix, etc)

- ❑ I want to purchase a ready-made template (WordPress)

- ❑ I want to find a template and I'm okay with customizing it myself (WordPress, Wix, Weebly, Squarespace, etc)

- ❑ I want to find a template and pay a virtual assistant or freelancer to customize it for me.

Remember to record your costs on the *Website Recurring Expenses Worksheet* in Step 2.

Web Design Final Cost: $_____

Step 4: Your Website Pages

The colors, logos, fonts, etc., that you use for your website are all great, but ultimately what draws traffic to your website is your content. You want every page on your website indexed by search engines so that readers can easily find you.

Those pages should reflect an author who is well worth a reader making an effort to add to their bookshelf. Now a website can constantly grow over time, but let's take a look at some pages you should have on your website before it's launched.

Home Page

A home page is the landing site for your website. Your latest book release should be a focal point when visitors enter your site. This may be a good place to add a few brief endorsements or blurbs.

In order to fit a lot into this space, some websites use large slideshows. If you do use slides, don't use too many. Three is probably a good number. No one is going to sit there all day staring at the slides.

If you have a blog as a part of your website (I will discuss more in Step 6), it's a good idea to show fresh content or your most recent blog posts.

About/Media Kit Page

Your "About" page should help people get to know you. Not only should it be factual and informational, but it should be personality driven. People should get a sense of who you are, what you stand for and a sense of your personality. Some points to consider:

- ❏ Briefly talk about your background and how you got started writing.

- ❏ Have you won any awards? Let people know!

- ❏ Be personal in a free flowing way. You don't want to sound too formal.

- ❏ Definitely don't include TOO much personal information. It's the internet, and you have to use common sense.

- ❏ Sometimes it's a good idea to include a short bio and a long bio on your about page.

The goal is for your potential readers to have a sense of what you are about. In this day of reality TV and social media, people really want to connect.

Journalists, bloggers, and other media often search for your media or press kit for quick information about you. You can add a media kit as a page on your website, or some authors like to create a downloadable electronic press kit (usually PDFs).

If you decide you want to add a media kit, some items you want to make available in your electronic media kit is:

❑ High resolution jpeg of yourself

❑ High resolution jpegs of your book covers

❑ A downloadable one sheet with quick facts about you

❑ Suggested interview questions are also helpful

Notice that I used the term high resolution when I referred to graphics. This means the jpeg should be at least 300 dpi (print size) or I like to tell authors to make sure the photo is at least 1500 in width. The larger the photo, the better options you're providing the person using the photo. They can resize or crop the photo without distorting the image.

Anyone can take a photo with their smartphone or tablet, but to ensure that you have a high resolution photo, you should consider working with a professional photographer. Plus, a great photographer will be able to get the lighting, the posture, the angle, and everything else right to give you an image that really shines. Remember, the photos you take can be used on your website banner, your "About" page and as your main avatar for social media profiles.

Before I talk about the next page on your website, I had one pet peeve about photos I need to address. Be sure to change the filenames for your photos and book covers.

Oftentimes graphics have the filename the camera or graphic designer assigned to them. Don't send media jpegs with filenames that look like this NCD2783971.jpg. How does that jumble of letters and numbers identify you?

Make it easy for a media person to locate your graphics after they download them by taking the time to rename photos with Yourname.jpg or YourBookTitle.jpg. I don't want to get too much into data management because that can take a whole chapter, but keep a dedicated folder on your computer, email or in a cloud system (Google Drive, Dropbox, Microsoft One Drive) where you can easily access promotional materials.

In fact, you can use a cloud system for dual purposes. For my electronic press kit, I provide a link to a shared folder on my Google Drive. I discovered that this was easier for me. Anytime I have new photos or new book covers, I upload them to the folder. Here is a link to mine: http://bit.ly/TyoraMoodyEPK

Notice, I went the extra step of creating a short URL. You can use bit.ly or goo.gl/ shortener URLs to track the number of clicks.

Books Page

You will be amazed how this page on an author website can sometimes be the most outdated content. I have gone to author's websites who have at least 1-2 books that have been released, but you can't find any information on the book page, not even the book cover.

Be sure you have a nice size image of all your book covers along with:

❒ Book synopsis

❒ Release Date

❒ ISBN

❒ Endorsements or reviews

❒ Excerpts

❒ Discussion questions for book clubs

If available, it doesn't hurt to include links to the e-book version or audiobook version too. Remember it's best to link directly to the book order page. Don't link to Amazon.com and expect a reader to search for your book. Go to the book page and copy the URL from your browser window.

If you plan to post the link on social media, you may want to use the short URL by looking for the share buttons on the Amazon page.

Usually, the Amazon short URL looks like this:

http://amzn.com/B00D6IRN3A

The mixture of numbers and letters are the ASIN number.

http://www.amazon.com/Trouble-Eugeena-Patterson-Mysteries-ebook/dp/B00D6IRN3A/ref=zg_bs_6190464011_2

You can also quickly find the URL, by clicking the "share" area located on the right side of the order page.

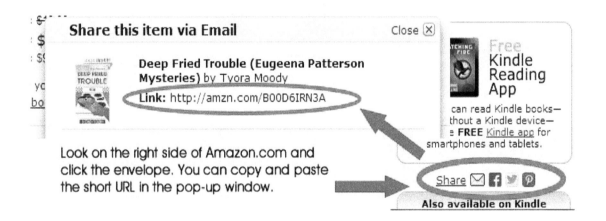

I do realize that I'm using Amazon as the example here, but please include links to all the major online booksellers that have your book in stock. The other online booksellers would appreciate the link and traffic.

Check to see if your book is available on:

- ❏ BarnesandNobles.com

- ❏ BooksAMillion.com

- ❏ Christianbook.com

- ❏ IndieBound.com

- ❏ Independent Bookstores

- ❏ Walmart.com

Add Your Own Store

Many authors like to offer autographed books for sale on their website. You might want to look into getting a PayPal account or set-up a merchant account via your bank. PayPal.com is probably the easiest to set-up, and they provide wizards under merchant services for creating shopping cart buttons. If you don't like using the PayPal buttons, you can use your own button. There are often two embed codes you can add to your website. If you understand how to add an HTML link to an image, use the code for email.

If you are going to be a vendor at an event, PayPal now offers a device to accept credit/debit card payments offline. The device easily attaches to your smartphone and can be used with an app. The other popular competitor for accepting offline transactions is Square.

If you want to be really fancy and provide a shopping cart experience, explore the websites below. I have split the list into simple and complex.

Simple Store Setup

A few books and products; quick to get up and running

- ❑ E-junkie - http://www.e-junkie.com

- ❑ Gumroad - https://www.gumroad.com

- ❑ Paypal - http://www.paypal.com

- ❑ Selz.com - https://selz.com

Complex Store Setup

Multiple books and products

- ❐ 1Automationwiz - http://www.1automationwiz.com

- ❐ 1ShoppingCart - http://www.1shoppingcart.com

- ❐ Clickbank - http://www.clickbank.com/

- ❐ Shopify - http://www.shopify.com

- ❐ Woocommerce (WordPress Plugin) http://www.woothemes.com/woocommerce

Events Page

Building relationships are essential and work even better when there is an opportunity for a face-to-face meeting. Consider adding a calendar or listing of upcoming events.

- ❐ So, what type of events should you include on your calendar?

- ❐ Do you have a book signing or a book release party?

- ❐ Are you visiting with a book club?

❏ Are there upcoming conferences where you will be speaking?

❏ Are you going to be a guest blogger?

❏ Are you going to be on TV, radio, or participating in a podcast?

While I spend a considerable amount of time talking about building and managing your online presence, your offline presence is a part of this book marketing pie too. Connecting with readers in person is something you don't want to miss out on doing, and you certainly want to let people know where they can find you. Since many writers are speakers, book club meetings, conferences and retreats are ideal places to be.

Speaking Opportunities: If you are an expert on a certain topic include a listing or link to a page of workshops and webinars that you're willing to present.

For Book Clubs: Be sure to reach out to book clubs via this page as well. If you're willing to Skype or travel to a location, let them know. Include a link to a speaking form so that book clubs or other organizations can request you for their speaking engagement.

Photos: Readers who you meet offline, like to see photos. The Event page would be a good spot to display photos. These days it's probably easier to post a link to your Facebook album or Instagram on your website

Contact Page

Some may argue with me, but the contact page is one of the most important pages on your website. You do NOT want to lose an opportunity for people to reach you. I can't tell you how often I receive interview requests for radio and blogs via the contact form on my website.

I recommend using forms on your contact us page versus an email address. You will save yourself the headache of having to deal with unwanted spam. There are special "robot spiders" that crawl the internet all the time looking to grab email addresses. Sounds like something from a science fiction novel, but I'm sure you have had your share of spam in your inbox.

My favorite place for building forms is Wufoo.com. Wufoo is great because they provide sample forms to help you get started and these are some beautiful forms. I also like the fact that all the data is stored so that you can refer to names and emails later. You can build up to three forms for free. The form can be a contact page, a registration page or even a survey.

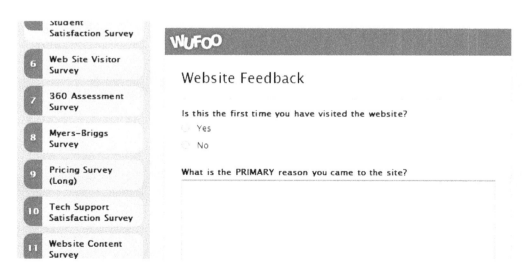

I also recommend getting a Gmail or Yahoo account. Yahoo and Gmail do pretty good jobs of catching spam. Keep your business email separate from your personal email.

Most purchased web hosting offer an option to forward or redirect yourname@yourdomain.com to your Gmail or Yahoo account. Check this out thoroughly because some web hosts will make you think you have to pay an extra fee for using their email servers.

Web Pages Checklist

Have you created the following pages for your website?

❏ Home Page

❏ About Page

- o Added a Bio

- o Take a professional photo

❏ Book Page

- o Added all my books with information (synopsis, ISBN, etc)

- o Provided ordering information

- o Added links to excerpts

❏ Events page

- o Added a calendar of upcoming events

- o If you're a speaker, added a listing of workshops

- o For book clubs, ways to book your for book club meetings

❏ Contact Page

Web Design Maintenance Checklist

After you launch your website, you should plan to create a maintenance schedule. This doesn't have to be every month, but at least a few times a year. Keep in mind if you have a blog attached to your website, you will probably be more aware of out-dated information.

Whether you pay a designer or DIY your website, remember to add a maintenance schedule to your calendar. Ideally you should plan to update a website with every new book release or at least quarterly.

Quarterly

❏ Do you have new book releases? Add the book cover to the website at least 30-60 days before the release.

❏ Do you have new events to add to your calendar?

❏ Do you have photos from events to link to on Facebook, Instagram, etc?

Annually

❏ Does your bio need updating?

❏ Have you changed the copyright year at the bottom of your website?

Step 5: Building A Mailing List

You may have reached this part of the book and thought, wow, this is a lot of work. So, why is it so important to send readers to your website? This section will answer that question.

Capturing the email address of the people who land on your website is highly important to your marketing plan. With all the email a person receives, when they give permission to add their email address to your list, that's a great endorsement of trust in your author brand.

They want more of your books!

No matter how many fans you have, they are all important, and you want the ability to reach out to them in a direct way outside of social media. Don't get caught up in the idea that social media is the only way to market.

Email marketing is an incredibly valuable piece of your marketing plan.

You want to make sure the email addresses you are capturing are via a double opt-in process that allows the subscriber to confirm their subscription via email.

Never just add email addresses to your list without permission. You don't want to be labeled a spammer.

Subscription boxes are usually added in a highly visible place on your website and blog, most of the time near the top right. If you offer some type of feature, like free chapters, e-books, video or audio, people are usually more willing to add their email to your list in exchange for a freebie.

The key to building a list is so you can create a loyal group of readers interested in updates about your latest release. This is pretty crucial to future sales.

Planning a Newsletter

Of course, after you build your list, you want to plan to keep in touch with the subscribers. Many authors do monthly or quarterly newsletters. This is an opportunity to share a personal side with you as well as may direct readers back to your website for new information they missed.

Some popular mailing list platforms are:

- Aweber – http://www.aweber.com/

- Constant Contact – http://www.constantcontact.com/

- Mailchimp – http://mailchimp.com/

- Your Mailing List Provider – http://www.ymlp.com/

If you do plan to blog, email marketing can be an excellent way to promote your blog posts. WordPress.com/WordPress.org and Blogger.com offer ways for your blog readers to subscribe to your blog posts. Look for ways to give your subscribers options by either receiving blogs daily or weekly.

We will talk more about blogging in Step 6.

Building a List Checklist

Have you selected a mailing list provider (Mailchimp, Constant Contact, etc)?

❑ Yes

❑ No

If you need to pay a fee for your mailing list provider have you included the cost along with other recurring expenses?

❑ Yes

❑ No

What's the name of your mailing list provider:

_____

Have you added the opt-in or sign-up box in a visible place on your website?

❑ Yes

❑ No

Do you have social media posts or have you scheduled social media posts asking people to join your mailing list?

❐ Yes

❐ No

Do you have a freebie (free chapters, worksheet, etc) that you can give away for people to sign-up for your mailing list?

❐ Yes

❐ No

Have you set up a schedule for sending newsletters to your mailing list (monthly, quarterly, etc)?

❐ Yes

❐ No

Do you have a sign-up sheet ready to go when you're selling books at offline events?

☐ Yes

☐ No

Have you scheduled or planned for annual newsletters for the holidays (Christmas)?

☐ Yes

☐ No

Newsletter Ideas

On the next few pages, record topics you can email to your newsletter subscribers for the next 12 months. Use the monthly worksheets and your favorite calendar to work out a schedule for the newsletter.

It's okay, if you can't do monthly newsletters, but take a look at your upcoming book release schedule, events, etc and be sure to plan newsletters around those events.

_____

_____

_____

_____

_____

_____

_____

_____

_____

Newsletter Ideas This Month

JANUARY 20_____

Newsletter Ideas This Month

FEBRUARY 20_____

Newsletter Ideas This Month

MARCH 20_____

_____

_____

_____

_____

_____

_____

_____

_____

_____

_____

_____

Newsletter Ideas This Month

APRIL 20_____

_____

_____

_____

_____

_____

_____

_____

_____

_____

_____

_____

Newsletter Ideas This Month

MAY 20_____

Newsletter Ideas This Month

JUNE 20_____

Newsletter Ideas This Month

JULY 20_____

Newsletter Ideas This Month

AUGUST 20_____

Newsletter Ideas This Month

SEPTEMBER 20_____

Newsletter Ideas This Month

OCTOBER 20_____

Newsletter Ideas This Month

NOVEMBER 20_____

Newsletter Ideas This Month

DECEMBER 20_____

_____

_____

_____

_____

_____

_____

_____

_____

_____

_____

_____

Step 6: Business of Blogging

After you create your website pages, you still have another issue. As beautiful as those pages may appear, they are static pages that change at the most a few times a year. The key to continuous traffic to your website is creating content that attracts readers more than a few times a year.

I've been a blogger for over a decade and blogging continues to be the most consistent traffic generator.

Should I Have a Blog?

I often get this question. If you have a certain niche or topic, a blog offers a great way to attract an audience to your website on a consistent basis. At the core of your book marketing, you have to understand that generally, people are online to find information or something new to read. They're looking to fill a need with available content.

You may or may not have heard the term "content is king." In recent years, there is a movement among internet marketers that has been coined "Content Marketing." The Content Marketing Institute states, "Content marketing is a marketing technique of creating and distributing relevant and valuable content to attract, acquire, and engage a clearly defined and understood target audience – with the objective of driving profitable customer action."

There is often a website with a very robust blog at the center of content marketing. Marketers are continuously driving traffic back to their websites where the goal is to capture a new lead or customer. This type of marketing is a bit different from social media marketing. Many authors spend a lot time posting "Buy My Book, Buy My Book" messages on Facebook or Twitter, but it's obvious they're more interested in getting the sales and/or commission.

Now don't get me wrong if you put a lot of effort into a book, you want to see some profit. As a literary entrepreneur, we should be marketing with the "How This Book Can Serve Your Needs" to our readers. Whether the reader has a desire to improve a skill, be inspired or just to have a story that carries them away from the world for a few hours, we want our brand and books to be appealing.

Having a blog with valuable content builds credibility and professionalism. Your website will truly become a marketing tool that draws visitors. The more people who visit your website, the odds of acquiring new readers increase significantly.

Does the thought of coming up with a blog posts every day strike fear into you? I mean you're an author, and you want to only write books. Books are more tangible because you know people can buy your paperback from the bookstore or download your e-book.

What can blogging do to bring me money?

Let's ask another question. A better question!

How do people find my book to purchase?

There has to be a consistent way to draw traffic to your book and your author brand. Remember, you don't want to be a salesperson. Having a blog can serve as an excellent website companion for building an online platform. Your website is your stomping ground where you can keep all kinds of goodies for your visitors. Those goodies can come in the package of a blog with quality content.

Tools for Blogging

If you are looking to set-up a blog, keep in mind the Web hosting solutions I discussed earlier in this book all provide blogging platforms. They are listed again below:

- Blogger – http://www.blogger.com
- Squarespace – http://www.squarespace.com
- Weebly – http://www.weebly.com
- Wix – http://www.wix.com

- WordPress – http://www.wordpress.com

Getting Started

Okay, so you have set-up a blog, and that old fear is slipping back. Why did I set this up? What do I have to talk about? Now before you start whining, you don't have anything to write about for a blog, let's do some brainstorming.

The biggest mistake I see newbie bloggers make is trying to make the blog all about them. I'm sorry, but at some point, you're going to run out of stuff to write, and most of us are NOT all that interesting. I'm just saying!

Are you still feeling daunted or overwhelmed by the idea of writing small blog posts on a regular basis? Here are some other ideas to help you jump into the world of blogging.

Interview Authors and/or Post Book Reviews. This is where a lot of authors start with blogging. Reach out to fellow authors in your genre or in other genres.

For example, on my WrittenVoicesBlog.com, I feature other Christian fiction and nonfiction authors.

Video Blogging. If writing daily or several times a week for a blog doesn't appeal to you, you might consider video blogging. Videos are really easy to create these days via a webcam or your smartphone camera. Setting up a YouTube channel that shares your blog name is a great way to grab traffic. Google owns YouTube and Google loves bloggers. Why not combine both worlds so that you can get a high ranking on Google?

These days you can easily use Facebook Live or Periscope to connect with your readers. Download and store those videos to use on your website's blog for people who missed your live broadcast.

Group-Authored Blogs. Another alternative is to start a blog with a group of writers or authors. Each contributing writer can be assigned one day a week (or month) to add a blog post. Some existing group-authored blogs may offer guest blog opportunities.

Guest Blogging. Keeping up with a blog is hard work. Because life happens, many bloggers open their blogs up for guest blogging. Be on the lookout for opportunities or query blog owners to ask if they would be interested in posting guest bloggers. A blog with high traffic can be a win-win for your blog if you provide quality content. Be sure to include your website/blog URL in a brief bio so that people can find out more information about your author brand.

5 Traffic Building Tips

Let's make sure you are meeting your main goal – to attract readers. It makes no sense to set-out on a blogging journey, and you're not making proper use of your blog.

I want to first make sure you understand these days, blogging is a **business model**.

1. Use call-to-actions

I have been to blogs that authors have set-up, and their books are nowhere to be found. It's one thing to bring people to your blog, but you need prominent call-to-actions for their eyes to view.

❏ Is your latest book release visible on the top or side of your blog?

❏ Is there a link to more info OR an excerpt OR an order page?

Is your blog connected to your website, where readers can click to view more about you and even more importantly, the "books" page? I HIGHLY RECOMMEND that your blog be a part of your website's navigation.

2. Write quality, evergreen blog posts

A few years back, it was recommended to blog daily or at least three times a week. That's not reasonable and not even a good plan. It's probably why many bloggers crash and burn.

Learn SEO. It's more important for search engine optimization (SEO) for you to write quality posts. If you can create a post that is evergreen, meaning they're perpetually good at any time to read and will not get dated. Your reader should walk away and feel like they've learned something new or gained a new perspective they can consider using. Pay attention to keywords and learn the basics of SEO.

Study Your Audience. Use SurveyMonkey.com or Google Drive Forms to create a short survey for your audience. Find out what they want to know that you can provide. Don't be afraid if other people are doing the same thing. I have found that certain people like to get the information from whom they most admire. That person could be you.

Evaluate. Be sure to evaluate how your blog posts are doing. You should definitely add Google Analytics to your website. This is a powerful free tool that may give you more information than you care to know, but taking the time to dig into how many people visit your website, which pages are popular, etc., is really helpful. If you're getting spikes in traffic, consider why that particular blog post was popular with your audience and plan to write related posts.

3. Post to social networks.

If you use WordPress, you can install plugins that push out links to your blog posts as soon as they are published. The Wordpress.com JetPack plugin is my favorite.

Here is also where you want to use social media tools like Hootsuite.com or BufferApp.com to schedule posts. Remember, there's nothing wrong with posting the link to your blog post more than once on social networks. Just space out the posts on different days and times.

For example, after I publish a blog post, I will schedule to post a few days after and then again in a month.

4. Make blog posts easy to share.

I can't tell you how often I come across a really good post and there are no easy ways to share. Always include social media icons on your blog that allow readers/visitors to easily share your blog posts on Facebook, Twitter, Google Plus, etc. People who read your blog regularly become influencers when they choose to share, so make it easy.

Both blogger.com and wordpress.com have excellent social media sharing tools. If you use WordPress.org (self-hosted), I want to highly recommend activating the Wordpress.com JetPack plugin that usually comes automatically installed on most webhosts. I slept on this plugin for a few years until I realized some of the neat things it offers.

5. Make blogging a part of your marketing plan.

I talked about guest blogging on high-traffic blogs in your area of interest, but there are other ways to draw attention to your blog.

Article marketing or Re-publishing. Re-purpose some of your blog posts into articles and submit them to popular directories like EzineArticles.com. In the past few years, websites like Medium.com and the social network platform, LinkedIn.com allow for publishing on their platforms. Depending on your topic, you can attract even more traffic. Be sure you include ways for readers to visit your website.

Content Upgrades. Remember earlier I mentioned that building a mailing list is probably the most important part of your marketing plan. You could combine blog posts to create a free e-book. Or keep it simple. Create a checklist, cheat sheet or worksheet related to your blog post for readers to download in exchange for their email.

You can view examples at:
http://theliteraryentrepreneur.com/category/freebies/

Blogging Brainstorming Worksheet

Are you still trying to figure out what to blog? Blogging does require passion. Use the following questions to help you brainstorm.

Who are the characters in your books? Do they have interesting tie-ins to real-life professions, situations or events?

_____

_____

_____

_____

Do you have a lot of historical, medical or scientific research that you can share?

_____

_____

_____

_____

Do you have a certain niche or topic that you write about in your books that give you credibility as an expert? Workshop facilitator? Conference speaker? List some of your workshops or other topics below.

_____

_____

_____

_____

Are there updates, breakthroughs, new discoveries or current events that relate to your book?

_____

_____

_____

_____

What have you learned from your personal publishing journey? How did your book design process work out for you? What did you learn about the editing process?

_____

_____

_____

_____

Are there other authors in your genre you can feature or interview? Don't be afraid to cross-promote.

_____

_____

_____

_____

Can you provide a solution to a problem or an issue?

Blogging Checklist

Is your blog connected to your website, where readers can click to view more about you and even more importantly, the "books" page?

❏ Yes

❏ No

Are your most recent blog posts visible from your website home page or side bars?

❏ Yes

❏ No

Is your most recent book(s) visible in the sidebar of your blog?

❏ Yes

❏ No

Do you have an editorial calendar?

❏ Yes

❏ No

Do you have consistent posting times? (Ex. 2-3 times a month).

❏ Yes

❏ No

If yes, how many times do you plan to publish a blog post?

_____

Do you have auto-posting setup to Twitter, Facebook and other social networks from your blog?

❏ Yes

❏ No

Are you scheduling your blog post more than once in a social media management tool?

☐ Yes

☐ No

Have you added social media sharing to your website pages or blog?

☐ Yes

☐ No

Do you have your mailing list sign-up in a visible place on your blog?

☐ Yes

☐ No

Blog Post Ideas

On the next few pages, record topics you can blog about over the next 12 months. Use the monthly worksheets and your favorite calendar to work out a schedule for the topics.

_____

_____

_____

_____

_____

_____

_____

_____

_____

_____

Blog Posts JANUARY 20_____

Blog Posts FEBRUARY 20_____

Blog Posts MARCH 20_____

Blog Posts APRIL 20_____

Blog Posts MAY 20_____

Blog Posts JUNE 20_____

Blog Posts JULY 20_____

Blog Posts AUGUST 20_____

Blog Posts SEPTEMBER 20_____

Blog Posts OCTOBER 20_____

Blog Posts NOVEMBER 20_____

Blog Posts DECEMBER 20____

Step 7: Social Media Connections

Yes, I saved social media as the last step. From Steps 1-6, it has been all about building on a foundation.

There is no argument that the best form of advertisement is word of mouth. When you spend time building relationships using social media platforms, you have the potential to attract a readership or influencers for your book.

Social networks are constantly changing. When I started getting into social media in 2007, MySpace.com was still pretty popular. Now Facebook.com has been pretty dominant for several years now. Following right behind Facebook at the top are YouTube and Twitter. Some social networks that grew super fast are Pinterest and Instagram.

I always encourage clients not to become overwhelmed by all the platforms, but start engaging on two social networks or even one. When you create social media accounts, please make sure you fill - out the profiles completely by including the link to your website. Remember, your website is the hub.

Also, be sure to use social media icons to add your social media profiles to your website. If someone comes to your website, you want to encourage them to LIKE your Facebook page or follow you on Twitter.

Let me make this real clear! Social media can bring you sales, but you're mainly connecting on social media to expose your books to potential readers, especially those who are a part of your target audience. The strongest way to build your platform is utilizing these free tools. Ultimately, it is how well your author brand is built that determines your longevity in the book business. If you continue to publish quality books and stay consistent in connecting with new readers, your rewards for hard work will come.

Social Media Checklist

What social media platforms have you signed up for?

Check off your social media platforms and write your *handles/usernames* for future reference below.

❑ Facebook: _____

❑ Twitter: _____

❑ Google+: _____

❑ LinkedIn: _____

❑ Pinterest: _____

❑ Instagram: _____

❑ Periscope: _____

❑ Snapchat: _____

Have you selected which 2-3 social networks above you will consistently post on each week?

❑ Yes
❑ No

If yes, which social networks:

1. _____

2. _____

3. _____

Have you selected a social media management tool (Hootsuite, Buffer, etc)?

❏ Yes

❏ No

If you need to pay a fee for a social media management tool (Hootsuite, Buffer, etc) have you included the cost along with other recurring expenses?

❏ Yes

❏ No

Have you added your social media links to your website?

❏ Yes

❏ No

Have you added social media sharing to your website pages or blog?

❏ Yes

❏ No

Have you connected your mailing list provider to your social media so your newsletter can be easily auto-posted when published?

❏ Yes

❏ No

Have you signed up for a image creation tool like canva.com for creating your own graphics?

❏ Yes

❏ No

Social Media Posts

On the next few pages, record topics you should consistently post to social media. You may want to use your favorite Word processor or spreadsheet to type the posts in advance. This makes it easy to copy and paste to your social media management tool.

_____

_____

_____

_____

_____

_____

_____

_____

_____

Note from the Author

You've made it through the end of the workbook, I hope along the way you have been building your website and considering blogging as a business model. A website is an evolving project. It's like your home; there are always projects to do or maintain. If you like this workbook, **please share a review**.

I would love to see your author website. Please do share your website with me. You can send your website to info@theliteraryentrepreneur.com or tag me on:

- Facebook (The Literary Entrepreneur)
- Twitter (@TLEonline)
- Instagram (@literaryentrepreneur)

I also want to encourage you to visit TheLiteraryEntrepreneur.com and sign up for *Inside the Toolkit* newsletter. This is a newsletter filled with book marketing advice from myself and other literary entrepreneurs.

If you would like downloadable worksheets for future planning, visit the library at http://theliteraryentrepreneur.com/join/

Many blessings on your literary journey!

Tyora Moody

About the Author

Tyora Moody is the author of Soul-Searching Suspense books which include the Reed Family Novellas, Eugeena Patterson Mysteries, Serena Manchester Series, and the Victory Gospel Series. She is also the author of the nonfiction book, *The Literary Entrepreneur's Toolki*t, and the compilation editor for the Stepping Into Victory Compilations under her company, Tymm Publishing LLC.

As a literary-focused entrepreneur, she has assisted countless authors with developing an online presence via her design and marketing company, Tywebbin Creations LLC. Popular services include virtual event planning, book covers and book trailers.

To contact Tyora about book club discussions or for book marketing workshops, visit her online at TyoraMoody.com or The LiteraryEntrepreneur.com.

www.ingramcontent.com/pod-product-compliance
Lightning Source LLC
Chambersburg PA
CBHW060153060326

40690CB00018B/4099